The stories at this level

Although the stories are still short, the languag
complex at this level. There are more v
well as phrases which express humo
than just telling the 'plot' of the story. S
may not be fully understood by the chi ... the
feeling of the whole story which is impo ... dual parts.

After reading the story, encourage your chi ... tell you in their own words what happened. Discuss the different characters and find out which ones your children most identified with and liked best, or which characters they most disliked, or thought were the funniest, or the most evil, or the naughtiest, etc. Your children will begin to identify with the characters and their emotions as well as following the plot. Consider 'acting out' the story; children love to role play stories with their friends (and themselves) anyway, without your suggesting it. Watch to see if this is happening. Do not hurry on to the next book.

You may feel that your child is memorising the words rather than 'decoding' them. This is fine; the activities at the end of the book will help develop gradual awareness of the patterns of individual words and letter formations. Your child should make some attempt, however, to read new words independently. If your child is successful with a word that hasn't been met before, you should give plenty of praise.

If a particular word is causing a problem, supply it, so that the flow of the story is kept going. Mistakes will be made, but this is a good sign, because it shows that your child is willing to try. Above all don't stop the reading in mid-stream to correct any mistakes. Wait until the end of a page or so, and then say 'Let's look at that bit again' and read it yourself, perhaps pointing out the words that were mistaken. Link the reading of several stories by pointing out the same words when they re-occur in a new story. Also point out labels, notices, signs etc. which they can see in everyday life.

Remember it is totally wrong to think that learning to read always means going on to more and more difficult books. Encourage your child to keep reading books from the earlier levels, and so build up confidence in tackling books alone. Get your children library tickets and encourage them to make their personal choice of the books they want to read – these will be mainly picture books which can be 'read' easily with great pleasure and satisfaction.

The activities at this level

All the activities are now intended for your child to do alone, although your interest and participation are always valuable. Some activities will involve writing. If there are any difficulties here, get your children to tell you what they want to write. Then you write it down first, so that it can be copied and read back by the children. Make the point that somebody's *writing* is intended to be *read*, just the same as a printed book is *writing* to be *read*.

Some of the activities require reasoning, which may need help from you. For example, the difference between what is 'true' and 'not true' may need clarifying. Don't worry if this proves a problem, as reasoning is more difficult than the straight reading of a story. Say what *you* think; it is very important that your child should approach reading in an active and questioning way, and thereby learning that there are very few completely right or completely wrong answers.

Your children might like to build up a 'Book of things I have done from my stories'. This would give a sense of achievement and permanence, as well as enabling you to keep a check on their development and what has been done.

When all the activities have been done, encourage your child to read the story again before moving on to another book.

The witch at Number 3

by Helen Arnold

Illustrated by Tony Kenyon

A Piccolo Original
In association with Macmillan Education

It was the morning of Friday the 13th.
Tamla was drawing.
She was drawing a witch.
She drew a witch with a pointed hat and a big black cat.
Suddenly Tamla stopped drawing.

There was a noise next door at Number 3.
The noise was a bit like a bump and
a bit like a creak.
"Number 3 is empty," Tamla said
to herself.
"Nobody has lived there for months.
I'd better go and see who's there."

Tony and Anna heard the noise too.
They came out to see who was there.
"Did you hear that noise?" said Tamla.
"Yes," said Anna. "It was a bump."
"No," said Tony. "It was a creak."

3

Then they all saw the black cat on
the doorstep of Number 3.
"It looks like the cat in my drawing,"
said Tamla.
"It looks like a witch's cat,"
said Anna.

3

Now they heard some strange music
coming from the house.
"What's that music?" said Tony.
"It sounds very odd," said Anna.
"I don't like it," said Tamla.
"I'm going home!"
So Tamla ran back home, and
so did Anna and Tony.

The witch at Number 3

Tamla went back to her drawing.
"There must be a witch at Number 3,"
she thought.
"A witch and a cat."
So she wrote *The witch at Number 3*
under her picture.

The next day there was no sign of the witch at Number 3.
Tamla went to see Liz and Len at Number 1.
She told them all about the bumps, and about the black cat, and about the odd music.

"Let's get Tony and Anna and make a plan," said Len.
So they made a plan to catch the witch.
"We must make a brew," said Liz.
"Then the witch will smell it and come out and see."

So they made a brew in the garden.
They were not sure what to put in it but they knew it must be nasty.
They put in some old paint water, a dead spider and a very old sock.
They put in one of Top's old bones and a rotten onion.
It smelt awful.

They saw the back door of Number 3
open just a crack.
The witch was coming out with
her black cat.
But she didn't look like a witch at all.
She didn't sound like a witch either.
"Hello," she said. "What a smell!
Who is making a brew?"

"Are you the witch?" said Tamla.
"No. I'm Mrs Brown. I've just moved in."
"Hello, Mrs Brown," said Tamla's Mum.
"May the children have some cake and a drink?" said Mrs Brown.
"It would be nicer than their brew," said Mrs Singh.
So they all had cake and lemonade in the garden.

The witch at Numb

"Do you think Mrs Brown is a witch?"
said Anna.
"She does have a black cat and she did come out when she smelt the brew,"
said Liz.
"If she's a witch, she's a good witch,"
said Tamla.
And they all agreed.

Things to talk about

1. Did you guess why there were all those noises coming from Number 3?

What would you do to welcome a new neighbour?

2. If you wanted to make a brew, what sort of things would you put into it?

Looking at pictures and words

1. Which of the sentences below are true? Which are not true?

Tamla drew a black cat.

Mrs Brown was a witch.

The brew smelt lovely.

Number 3 was empty.

2. Draw the things that were in the brew.
Write the names of the things under your pictures.

3. Can you make a list of all the noises in the story?

4. Here are some words from the story. Can you copy them, and fill in the missing letters?

n__ __se   cr__ __k   bla__ __   __ __mps

p__ __nted   gard__ __   wi__ __h   on__ __n

5. Here are some pictures from the story.
Can you copy the pictures and write under each picture what is happening?

Tamla is_____________. They are_____________.

Mrs Brown is___________. Tamla is___________.

6. Find the sentence which does not fit with the story.

Tamla went back to her drawing.

"There must be a witch at Number 3," she thought.

"A witch and a cat."

The dog was asleep.

So she wrote "The witch at Number 3" under her picture.

Now try this one. Which sentence does not fit?

They put in some old paint water, a dead spider and a very old sock.

They put in a worm and some old cake.

They put in one of Top's old bones and a rotten onion.

Things to do

Draw a picture of a witch, and write a story about the witch in your picture.

These activities and skills:	will help your children to:
Looking and remembering	hold a story in their heads, retell it in their own words.
Listening, being able to tell the difference between sounds	remember sounds in words and link spoken words with the words they see in print.
Naming things and using different words to explain or retell events	recognise different words in print, build their vocabulary and guess at the meaning of words.
Matching, seeing patterns, similarities and differences	recognise letters, see patterns within words, use the patterns to read 'new' words and split long words into syllables.
Knowing the grammatical patterns of spoken language	guess the word-order in reading.
Anticipating what is likely to happen next in a story	guess what the next sentence or event is likely to be about.
Colouring, getting control of pencils and pens, copying and spelling	produce their own writing, which will help them to understand the way English is written.
Understanding new experiences by linking them to what they already know	read with understanding and think about what they have read.
Understanding their own feelings and those of others	enjoy and respond to stories and identify with the characters.

First published 1988 by Pan Books Ltd,
Cavaye Place, London SW10 9PG

9 8 7 6 5 4 3 2 1

Editorial consultant: Donna Bailey

British Library Cataloguing in Publication Data
Arnold, Helen
The witch at Number 3.—(Read together.
Level 6).
I. Title II. Series
428.6 PE1119
ISBN 0-330-30227-2

Printed in Hong Kong